THE CARDINAL ACADEMY

AF375245

Welcome to the "Land of Letters"

Once upon a time, in the
Land of Letters, there lived
5 vowel sisters: **A, E, I, O, and U**.
The vowels had 21 brothers, called
Consonants. They were **B, C, D,
and G etc.**

However, the vowel sisters were very
mischievous in nature and would
always get into trouble.

These vowels sisters were special because consonants formed words with the help of vowels.
The sisters occasionally refused to assist their consonant brothers make words. Thus, consonants could only generate few words alone without vowels in them.

When they helped, their sisters
always demanded a favour, and
consonants always agreed.
Together, they made everything in
the Land of Letters come to life!

A E I O U

One sunny day, the vowel sisters went to play in the enchanted forest without informing anyone. They entered the forest for the first time. The sisters were excited to see the lush green trees, the colorful flowers, and the charming sounds of the birds chirping.

Vowels began to play and enjoy themselves in the forest. They lost track of the time.

As the sun began to set and the forest grew darker, the sisters started to get scared. They held each other and started calling out for help, but no one could hear them.

Back in the Land of Letters, the consonants—B, C, D, and the others—noticed that the vowel sisters were not seen anywhere. The consonant brothers began to worry about their missing sisters. Despite their sisters troublesome behaviours, the brothers loved their sisters and decided to go in search of them.

The brothers rushed into the forest in search of their sisters. Despite the fact that they were scared, they decided to bravely search for their sisters. Because they always knew that **"Unity is Strength,"** there was no doubt in their minds. They could overcome any challenge as a team.

a
e
i
o
u

They finally found their sisters. Consonants were happy to see them again. They decided to return but found themselves lost in the shadowy woodland. The letters were very sacred in the dark forest.

Just when they thought they couldn't escape, a kind fairy appeared before them.

She was a beautiful fairy with wings that could make her fly. The consonants and vowels were amazed to see the fairy in the dark forest.

"The vowel his gift,
the vowel be trea
with a will be treated
in honor a word we
begins with your sounds."

The letters asked the kind fairy to help, and she was willing to help them to get back home.

"I can help you all get out of the forest," the fairy said, "but there is one condition. The vowel sisters must now promise to assist their brothers. They must use their magical sounds to form words with consonants and work together."

The vowel sisters, feeling guilty for causing so much trouble, agreed right away. They knew their brothers only came into the forest to help them, and now they wanted to make things right.

They agreed to help consonants to make words always.

The fairy smiled and said to the sisters that "You will be appreciated and remembered from today onwards because you understood your mistakes and have agreed to help your brothers." Accepting responsibility for one's mistake is the first step towards improvement.

Fairy happily said,
"I appreciate the vowels sisters for agreeing to correct their mistakes and consonant brothers to come inside my enchanted forest to help their sisters though they were scared. So I will grant you all blessings"

"With effect from this moment forward, whenever a noun begins with one of your vowel sisters, like a, e, i, o, and u the noun will be respected with 'an' and 'a' when it begins with a consonant."

The letters reached home safely with
the help of the fairy.
From that day forward, the vowel
sisters and consonants did not return
to the enchanted forest.
They worked together to make words
and help each other. The sisters
learned their lesson, and everyone
lived happily ever after on the Land
of Letters.

EHEEE E
THE
END

5 Vowels

a e i o u

21 Consonants

b c d f g h j

k l m n p q r

s t v w x y z

Vowels Usage With Respect

An apple 

An elephant

An igloo 

An octopus

An Umbrella 

Consonants Usage With Respect

A bag

A car

A dog

A goat

A fish

From the
"Land of Letters"

Thank you!